Underrated Provinces

Underrated Provinces

Joel Chace

MadHat Press
Cheshire, Massachusetts

MadHat Press
MadHat Incorporated
PO Box 422, Cheshire, MA 01225

Copyright © 2024 Joel Chace
All rights reserved

The Library of Congress has assigned
this edition a Control Number of
2024937941

ISBN 978-1-952335-82-2 (paperback)

Words by Joel Chace
Cover image: from *A Deluge*, Leonardo da Vinci (ca. 1517–1518)
Cover design by Marc Vincenz

www.MadHat-Press.com

First Printing
Printed in the United States of America

For Larissa, Logan, Brechyn, Tristan, Oana, Boone, and Ruby

Table of Contents

Mercy's Long Reach

A Once	3
A Lesson	7
A Province	10
A Hall	16
A Number	18
A House	22
A Trombone	24
A Town	31
A Library	39
A Torso	62

A Ship

[Its language starts to]	71
[Steerage. Once abandoned]	72
[Only that one on board]	73
[There's talk of]	74
[Gods suddenly on board, dust]	75
[From the unseen]	76
[Bedmates coupling or]	77
[The celestials stumble]	78
[They claim that whirling's]	79
[As usual, only the]	80
[They remember all]	81
[Golden gleam of]	82
[Beginning, always, as]	83
[Sun. Sea. Lazy,]	84
[Growing from sky downward,]	85
[Word comes down of a new]	86
[The three speak on What]	88
[Yet again, they file]	90
[As they fade into holy]	91

[To the crow's nest they're]	92
[O, to be undone seeing]	93
[On that other vessel, I opened]	94
[The bow angel and the stern]	96
[Seems there's a tunnel]	97
[They wonder about]	98
Acknowledgments	99
About the Author	101

Mercy's Long Reach

A Once

If only a just

once, just an even

                                                        hunch, ounce for the

nonce. Despite her self and

                        singsong, mercy's long

reach leads her past

                              geese on her lawn, ripples in

               the sand and in the beyond

water that lifts and pulls her

farther into a current of

words, language. Not singsong, but song.

A Lesson

She speaks the sentence. Then, a

                      student at the board writes,
                        In English, there are three

        to's. Next one, … *there are*
                three too's.

Finally, ... *three two's.*
Prof: "So, you see it?" Usual

silence.
"No one?"

Usual blankness.
Prof again: "And how about

these:
    'I watched my mother
exhale for the final time.' 'My

                    little boy looked up with his
        sad face, and smiled.'
                    'We saw fog spread

        across river flats.'"
                    Usual
        inscribing in notebooks.

A
Province

Where America's

                                          tin, and they skip
the previews. Union
members leave for

                space, after saying,
You've done for me, what?
Where her blues are wider

than his, and there's much more
room underground.
America's tin with a

hard right cross. High wire doesn't
work today: rolling abyss,
frozen pipes. Conference of

ailments: breakfast clowns,
evangelicals, several
dissonant strangers, a rural

red monstrosity, and
a profligate crooner, neat
as a suntan. Low sky

and light bones. They all
prefer the unruled, so
they make irony zones, liquid

rosaries, black pebble-circles,
impertinent woes,
seduction contracts, unlikely

proteins, and stairways to
the stars, of course. Nonetheless,
the march always ends their

featured gambit, though the
staunchest citizens, with
fistfuls of disclosures, still

flee to lawns in the wee
small hours. They clear
the way for fountains,

spread plausible nets under
the gargoyle's scales, and keep
   the tome fires burning.

               Curious how their gazes
                    turn upward into
               uncontested night, into an

         inaudible rush.
      O, *iota of home*. O,
          flickering exit

                lights. O, kindling on
              the chair, rifle on the
                  knee. O, one way

left. O, hard time dusk. O,
    great adagio, bruised
      rubato, snow falling

        against pines, underrated
        province, headlong reverie,
        firmament of all their eyes.

A Hall

Four sentences:
In truth, you won't
fall through. Homework weighs her

down, and her hands
are on trial, but her honor
will see her through. Happiness
can't exist when heads — drunk,

powerful, male — float
in a dark bar lounge. Mountain
close round; three snowflakes, then
a squall: love.
　　　　　　All four turned

vertical, hammered into
earth. Corners of a new
hall that rises. Great,
invisible hall: no longer

in the hole of history;
wide undergirding; drawbridge
down, portcullis
open; sun in the

courtyard, time
freed. Come
what, come may;
come Grendel.

A Number

5 isn't the answer, nor
is 7 the
answer, nor is 5
the answer. But the answer

might be 5 inside
a larger 5 inside a
larger 5, as Deem
painted them all.
Jehovah's
house in the wilderness, for which

He provided exact
instructions: sockets, 5;
pillars, 5; curtains,
5; altar, 5 cubits
long and wide; court,

                    exactly 5 cubits long.
                                    Little
              girl with quintan learns
                          to welcome her
            paroxysms: *When they stop,
                    I'll have five long days*

without them.
                Bedridden once
   again – diabetes – he
        nonetheless created
   My Egypt, with 5 slants
   of light cutting across that

                        huge grain elevator's
            concrete and steel.
                        There is a war
            against vice in Lancaster. I
            am going home to speak
                for vice.
                        Oil, to anoint

furniture in His small
wilderness home; and,
once more, Yahweh, eternal
Precisionist, dictated: sweet
cinnamon and sweet calamus,

of 250 shekels,
each; cassia and pure
myrrh of 500
shekels, each.
*Incense of
a New Church*, those gray-white

smoke tendrils wafting toward black
stacks and a distant
dirty blue sky. Yet,
nature was his first
subject, watercolor

flowers.
*The last mad
throb of red just
as it turns green; the
ultimate shriek
of orange calling*

*all the blues
of heaven
for relief
and support.* And
he died in

his bedroom
overlooking
his
mother's
garden.

A
House

In the old
midnight home.
Rooms – deep
green, blue,

ochre – lit
only by
moonlight since
everyone
is dead.
In
each iteration,

the dreamer,
now as old or
older than the
dead, finds
an object, picks it
up: this time, a

                                          photo framed behind
                                               glass, lunar
                                             shine darkening
                                          darkening the gone
                                                  faces.
                                                        Exactly
                                                      then comes

                     the flood: grief,
                          black in
           deepest black, submersion
         enveloped in submersion.
                              What
                             bubbles
                             up are

                          words, words of
                              a language
                             of sorrow and
                          fear.
                                 Although
                              the dreams do
                              keep ending.

A
Trombone

This one slides through sky – not
across, but through – slide
moving, slicing through,
reminding that sky is
membrane, delicate,
thin, membrane that can be
wounded by sound, and healed
by sound, sound closest to
the human voice. Berlioz:
*from religious accent, calm
and imposing …
to wild clamours of
the orgy.* 1468,
Bruges, trombonist as a
he-goat. That
gliding sweep around
the D & H tracks.
Cappy –
brakeman, union guy who voted
all five times for Debs, trombonist

with his small-town band – on top
of a boxcar.
All those
angel-trombonists birthed
during the Renaissance.
Richard Strauss: *never look
at the trombone section; that
only encourages them.*

Payment record, Hildesheim,
1428: *to the new
trombonist and bombard
player, for drink money.*
Locomotive heads into
the straightaway; engineer
glimpses Cappy's body

dropping into the deep,
right gulch.
Unless
all 76 are placed side
by side in just one
line, indignities will
occur: bruised necks; knocked-off
hats.
1535, Nuremberg. Albrecht

Glockenton the Younger inserts
a trombonist into his
miniature *Job, His Wife, and Two
Musicians*. Much amiss in
this painting. Four side panels. In one,
a Renaissance priest has just
stepped outside the church, perhaps
a house; a little skeleton
precedes him. In the
panel below, a gaunt man on
his deathbed; the mourners all
turn away; a woman
in the foreground laughs; a
boy, perhaps a skeleton, climbs
out the rear window. Bottom right,
two men lift a body in
a winding sheet; in the background,
a packed charnel house. Final
panel, a blindfolded woman
leads a procession of robed and
hooded acolytes.

A handcar dispatched
back to retrieve the corpse; but
a mile away from the accident,
Cappy walks toward the next
station. He'd landed on
his feet, and lives 50
more years.

Saqueboute perhaps
derives from *saquer*, to draw
out, as a sword from its scabbard.
Just as he comes through the arch,
instruments make great
rejoicing. Sackbuts and others
make such a din that if
a bird happens to fly
past, they make it fall from
the sky into the crowd.
1509,
Urbino, Castiglione's
joke: A Brescian in Venice, sees
a trombone and inquires how
the tubing can fit down the

human throat, as the slide
retracts from seventh to first
position.
1561, Spain and Mexico,
Philip II's order: *Because of the cost of
maintaining the present excessive number
of instrumentalists who consume their time
playing trumpets, sackbuts, and other kinds
of instruments, and because
very many of those reared simply
to sing and play on instruments
soon become lazy scoundrels, we
require a reduction in the
number of Indians who are now
permitted to occupy themselves
as musicians.*
In
the center of the painting, Job
covered in sores, sitting in the
mire or perhaps a patch
of ashes and holding his cupped
hands before him, his head slightly
inclined, so he stares just above

the heads of the three
persons nearby: his wife, arrayed
in 16th-century finery, her mouth
open as she looks down at
her man, and two musicians, a shawm
player, eyes closed, and a
trombonist gazing at Job. Background,
several clean, modest German
buildings, a small group of
citizens observing the scene
of suffering, or perhaps
not.
*We shall all be changed, in
a moment, in the twinkling
of an eye, at the last
trombone; for it shall sound, and
sound, and the dead shall be
raised incorruptible.*
But Job's wife? What
does she say to her husband? Or
does she sing along with the
instruments? Why a trombone? Is

this a song of solace? Or is this
when she recommends that Job curse
God and die, with musical
accompaniment? Or does she
make that O with her
mouth because
she foresees having
to bear another seven
sons and three
daughters as part
of Job's
restoration? And what
does Job think? Job,
the only
one
who seems to understand.
At
his end, hospitalized,
Cappy sees a line of seven red
lights, one beyond
the other, sliding
off into night.

A
Town

Along a two-mile
stretch it appeared, slowly at
first — barns, fields, houses, lawns at each
end — then more quickly — stores,
diners, offices meeting
at the center. Along the
entire line, a tension, a slight
and constant tugging, the whole
enterprise seeking to end
itself, to give itself back.
*Everyone has cut
down their trees. But not me, I
couldn't do it.*
And people,
moving in the meadows, yards, in
and out of door frames. This one
passes the pharmacy
window but turns back to
view the new display, a
photo of the bearded ones,
the town fathers. Half
of them or so identified,
great-grandfathers or great-

uncles of the very old or
recent dead.
Through the long night's
inferno, the valley turns
to ash, and not even the dead
will sleep here.
Rondout
Reservoir, completed
1951: Eureka,
Lackawack, Montela
flooded. Neversink Reservoir,
1953: Neversink,
Bittersweet submerged.
A
father, two little
sons, sit on the shore, watch
the luck of a nearby
fisherman. He casts, squats, then
tilts his head level
with the water. He must
see the filmy flash of each
trout right before he
jerks his line and fights it
in. Seven. Eight. Just
while the three of them
look on. The father
wonders if the other man

can also glimpse a church
spire, still-standing wall, round
silo roof.
*Public Meeting at
DEP Police 2nd
Precinct. This is a great chance
for County residents to
become more familiar
with our mission and our*
*people. At the same time, we
welcome the opportunity
to learn more about
the concerns of local
residents and ways that we can
serve them better. There is no
overriding agenda for
the meeting.*
On each side of
Main, a parallel — railroad
tracks and river, each tugging
with tension, the rails'
ringing warns everyone to
get away in time, while
the other's deep singing proves
that rivers know how

reservoirs are made.
Drowned Towns. Under Lake Lanier, Oscarville. Georgia. After the execution of three young, black men accused of raping and murdering a white woman, the Night Riders burn the town to the ground, thus obviating that problem in the near future when the flood waters come. St. Thomas, Nevada: *development-induced displacement*. During drought remains of the old hotel and ice-cream shop appear.
We're not moving in the direction of displacing fewer people. We don't have thoughtful policies that appreciate communities' sense of place. One of the things I find so interesting is a paradox. The

American West is a culmination of placemaking, but also of placelessness, of moving on to the next thing when necessity dictates it. When a family or a community plants fruit trees, that's a sign that they planned to stay for a long time. Some of the sadder things is when people talk about their orchards being ripped out. The rain thunders along with the thunder. She gazes out her window and believes she sees the day from behind a waterfall that will soon thunder and thicken until there is nothing else. Back in the hometown again, staring at that town fathers' photo. One leans toward his neighbor, moves his mouth soundlessly. Then they all begin to stir, some shifting about, some angry, some looking down, scuffing their shoes on the ground. Their faces brighten, eyes gleam, as they begin to change positions, making the names penned below the photo no longer match the figures above, bolting, jumping, whirling, until they freeze, each one out of position, stock still. *Do you see all these old places? We are the owner, but today we are homeless. We try to protest, but we cannot because they call you a terrorist. We are talking about 12,000 years. We saw the history here, but now our children will never see those dusty,*

                    beautiful caves.
      REMEMBER. DIKES ARE
SAFE AT PRESENT. YOU WILL
BE WARNED IF NECESSARY. YOU
          WILL HAVE TIME TO
              LEAVE. DON'T GET
EXCITED.
            The Takings : Vanport,
       Kowaliga, York Hill, Seneca
                       Village, Sousana, Derwent,
                          Ashopton, Hasankeyf
                       Curon, St. Thomas, Beerston,
                       Cannonsville, Rock Rift, Rock
                          Royal, Granton, Arena
                         Union Grove, Pepacton
                         (meaning "Marriage
                             of the Waters").
         They are getting closer. No
         powder to fire, anyhow.
         Yet there is a movement – their
            beards growing like masses
            of vines, clutching, snagging,
              obliterating faces,
            bodies, and sky, the whole
            space blotting black, then

so slowly coming
clear again — the
same space, the same
plot of ground clear
of any body or
face — only
the sky, the old
land, land of

the ancient bear
and fox — and
on the primeval
ground, shiny, but
already, always
old,
already,
always cracked,

only a
black,
lensed
box,
memory's
broken
eye. Now,
submerged.

A
Library

Nine granite ramps rise
to glass walls that
rise into snow. Come-and-go
constant visitors, mostly
from the circling-around
university. But not
all. Anything might happen
here. This child
runs up to her mother and
whispers, **I found a river
to fill your cup.** A river found
maybe in some book, maybe
flowing, barely visible,
beneath a black marble floor.
Hogarth: *You classical
archeologists, who have found
so much in Greece or in
Asia Minor, forget
this city.*
Lovers stroll, share
plush sofas, or lean against
each other in the stacks. One says,
**570 BCE, he
was born the same day she hurled
herself into the Aegean.**
The same moment, I wonder?

Pairs of lovers walk
suspended pathways between
floors. Walk and think: best
way. They speak about
thought. **Mind does not think
intermittently. What it
is to be intellect does
not lie in its being thought
by us.** When intellect thinks that
**existent thing that is an
intellect in actuality,
it does not think an existing
thing outside itself, but only
thinks itself in unconscious thought.**
Below that walkway, voices. Other
voices that drift up. Each voice drifting
up from a mouth, invisible,
below. Two lovers embrace in
a stairwell. On the step beneath them,
a dropped book – *Mouth Pieces* – has
landed on its spine and splayed open.
*Drifting up a stairwell, Mouth:
both its eyes, two ears, one hand, one
leg, with foot. Today it wishes
to say* **numbers**, *so it does,
thusly:* **numbers**. *Just the way it might
say* **lilacs**, *or* **way**.

"Why, Mouth, your eyes, ears,
appendages?" Head, face,
arm, hip need them no longer.
Now they are of
me: whereof I
speak; whatof I speak./////
Now Mouth is tired of answering.
This happens, since it was really
born to interrogate. Drifting,
again, in a stairwell, two eyes
observe, on a landing, two
lovers pressed against the railing.
What [are they]? What [do they do]? What
[physical space do they
[inhabit], [and] **where**? All other
unimportant questions
remain unasked./////
They ask Mouth how it was born.
Again, it says. "All right, how
were you born? **Again.** What
do you mean?" **Once more.**/////
Rising from what is best
known to what is unknown
in the unconscious.
Those on higher floors look out
into February
early-evening, liquid

violet light, over snow. Later,
they gaze at a night, snow shushing
against glass, snow that drifts down and
up, that could be ash drifting up, then
down, up from and back into
ravening flames invisible
below, ash lifting
free from books, parchments, scrolls, a
world vanishing in fire.
Out of the Library's ashes, she
rose, rises. Tenth Muse. Yet still
hurled, hurls herself from that high rock.
Lucan: *Nor did the fire fall
only upon the vessels: the
houses near the sea ignited
from the spreading heat, and
the winds fanned the conflagration,
till the flames, smitten by the eddying
gale, rushed over the roofs.*
Her death day, his birth
day. She made, from sacred
singing, new poetics. He
heard metal on metal
harmonies, took music's
heart, turned it into only
math. Legitimization
as distortion.

Here, it is possible, though not
painful to be lost. Passing:
long stacks, receding to
shadows; cases of open texts,
maps, daggers, goblets, astrolabes,
buttons, gloves; era after
era, under glass; era
rhyming with era. Then books left
on hundreds of tables. One
entitled *Times Rhyme*:
*They built reverence for inevitability
into the arches. But, oh, if only the elms
could have been saved. The mind does not know itself, except
in so far as it perceives the ideas
of the modifications of the body.* Consequently,
she refers to reason's rhyme and explains: **Immense, marvelous
golden wheels roll over me, each day more of them. They
turn me into light so I can study the timbre
of radiance.** *Her neighbors spent the whole afternoon
in her home but never once uttered the word*
condolence. *They maintained that every night the dead
entered their house and were roundly scolded, told they had
to return to their own moldy hostels. And they forced her to
choose: the cave is either the rock, or it is the hole.*/////
Standing with her left elbow against the cigarette
machine, she surveyed the tables. She asked if we'd
ever heard of that sort of rhyming before: what did she

*say it was called? It appeared to be summer. Eye
of the daisy. Out there, rain blinded the barren,
stuccoing it only, but as soon as he emerged from
that tunnel, they noticed the horror — mouth hole and
those hundreds of his hands. Of course, her father
was in one of his moods again. Out of
the ground, rising all day like a huge face.* / / / / /
The circling-around
university and the

circling-around city can
be here, inside glass walls that rise
into snow. White and yellow
windows — university's,
city's — become smears in wet
snow against glass. University,
city are here. Enclosed.

                 Hogarth
advised giving up on that
old city. But, with water
dripping, echoing: We
supposed old Alexandria
was destroyed, only
to realize that when you
stroll on the sidewalks, it
is just below your feet.
One cistern, three stories
deep. Egyptian, Corinthian,
Roman elements in the

arches constructed from
above-ground ruins. As much
cathedral as water supply.
*Underneath the streets and
houses, the whole city
is hollow.* One canal from the
great river carried flood water
into perhaps thousands
of immense chambers.

1842, the Croton
Aqueduct finally
brought clean water to
the city. From the Receiving
Reservoir to the
Distributing Reservoir — Fifth
Avenue between 40th
and 42nd, where
the Library now stands.
*Mouth enters — well, hops —
into the academy.
Long, lonely — well, empty —
corridors. Silence in
those hallways. Two ears hear
another silence: of ones who
don't wish to be found, to be
found out. The great hall is ornate,
unpeopled, terribly hushed.*

*Hand holds an unshelved book that
won't open. One after
another, books that won't open./////
Certain reservoir rocks used
for the foundation can still
be seen. Cornerstone, with relic
box, 11/10, 1902.
1897, John Shaw
Billings sketched floor plan
on a postcard. 16 years until
completion. Three floors.
$9,000,000. $20,000,000
for the plot.
Occasionally Mouth
wants nostrils, but knows
it can't have everything:
no chiming of resources.
Eyes, ears, hand, leg – enough. Though
one day hand picks up paper
money from pavement.
Mouth studies it closely, then
wonders, If I had another
hand, could one give
the other this money?
Mouth drops the bill, moves on.
Mouth wishes to
hug its own poverty./////
Most probably that library*

housed the entire of
Greek literature. *Demetrius
had at his disposal a large
budget in order to collect,
if possible, all the books
in the world; to the best
of his ability, he carried out
the king's objective.*
Carrère and Hastings designed
even the wastebaskets. Pink
Tennessee marble lions: Patience
and Fortitude. Opening day,
1911: very first
call slip, for Della Bacon's
Shakespeare study; text, not
catalogued. First book delivered,
seven minutes after
request, Nikolai Grot's
*Nravstvennye idealy
nashego vremeni,*
(Nietzsche and Tolstoy's
moral ideas).
*If he should suffer embarrassment, yet still believe,
and intercede for Zoar, and ask to be sent to the
city of safety, he will find a place where he cannot
rest on laurels, where it is too close and small for even
the best set of morals. Eye of day, or else true salt of*

earth. So what lies deep under the threads? He went out of his
mind while he was quite a young man and composed
continually in the asylum, using sheets
of music paper he had been using for a very
different purpose, saying with delight,
That's all the works of man are worth. If a person go on
analyzing names into words, and enquiring also
into the elements out of which the words are formed, and keeps
on always repeating this process, he who has to
answer him will at last give up the enquiry in despair.
But at what point ought he to lose heart? Must he not stop when
he comes to the names which are the elements of all other
names and sentences; for these cannot be supposed to be
made up of other names? The great bridge to the mainland:
she walks it, aware that gulls are flying beneath her feet./////
Here, picking up books left
by others on tables: beginning with
the exact pages left open.
Mouth: **Bridge.** And repeats. One
after another spills out
into a line at end of
which a tiny, sad Mouth stands and
looks back to realize that it
has crossed all the bridges
before coming to them./////
Here, any patron holds
an open hand

before a shelf's empty
space, and, like Athena sliding
palpably forth from air,
the searched-for book will
emerge. To the Mouseion
Ptolemy's heir appended the
Library, which held
an enormous collection
of scrolls, including all those
the government seized
for copying, from foreign ships.
In the *peripatos*, they
(research students, really)
strolled and conversed.
*Someone comes toward Mouth, and stops
to stare.*
I see the person
seeing me but cannot see
me seeing. And am I now
a mirror? – with a fine, finest
mesh draped before it?
Do I now take this mesh
into the mirror that I am?////
*The one leaving and the one staying. The one leaving
shifts, blurs, and returns, shifted, blurred. Part of the one
having left is left behind, or a small something is brought
back. The one having stayed must revise, must, because both
must eat. Inhabiting has to be a truth; permission*

has to be allowed. *Eyes meeting, pulling clarity
from another's mind. It is in the nature of reason
to perceive things under a certain form of
eternity. Inadequate and confused ideas
follow by the same necessity as adequate
or clear and distinct ideas. The case of language, you see,
is different; for when by the help of grammar we assign
the letters alpha or beta or any other
letters to a certain name, then if we add, or
subtract, or misplace a letter, the name which is
written is not only written wrongly, but not written
at all; and in any of these cases becomes other than a name.* / / / / /
Unlike the academy,
the Lyceum wasn't
private: often lectures were
free and open to anyone.
1919, one-story
lunchroom bungalow added to
southern courtyard, which became,
eventually, the staff's
social and recreational
center: plays, puppet shows,
readings, receptions, revues, an
historical pageant
ending with
dancing in the
main lobby.

Here, each night, some stay. Pull
together sofas or
arrange them into corrals. Spread
blankets they've brought. After those long,
wandering perambulations –
rest. Galaxies of flakes swirl
in darkness. They've picked up books
left by others on tables:
*In Alexandria, thoughts
of Olympus flickering
and few. Parabalani, the
archbishop's monk militiamen,
razed what remained of
the Library, ruined
pagan temples, Jewish
neighborhoods, then looked to
Hypatia, "the witch." Dragged her
from a chariot, stripped her, flayed
her skin with fragments
of oyster shells, dismembered
her, burned her. The new
religion's triumph.*
Mind
to Mouth: **I really need
a place more rarefied.** But
for one arm, one leg, scaling
that peak is brutal. They heave
up onto the summit, bloodied

and drained. Two ears hear a torrent of wind. Two eyes begin to scan the circular vista. Mind loves it up there — day after day, cold, cold clarity. Mouth: **What is that green expanse down there?** Mind: Nothing at all. Don't even think about it. But Mouth does, and days later: **I'm taking us all down.** And in that green field, Mouth announces, This is the Valley of Silliness./////
Mouth readies itself to speak and tells hand to carve each statement into a fallen twig.
I believe with certainty that I have one hand ... with certainty ... one leg ... two eyes ... two ears. And so much more. What with speaking and carving, time passes. But finally hand bends, twists, weaves all those twigs into the nest that Mouth calls **home**./////
Prairies don't apologize, but it turns out that angry banging on the piano keys actually can help. Or there's listening to Puccini while cabbage boils. This is

*what some call Pre-established Harmony, which removes
all notion of miracle from purely natural actions,
and makes things run their course in an
intelligible manner. Meanwhile, the promise-crammed air
and crocodile are still to come; blithe ass-grabbers wait
outside the theater. Rim keeps brightening. Each day
the world unfolds its miracles, its atrocities. He
was almost the ugliest man I'd ever seen – and yet
the force of his intellect was felt in every glance
of his eyes and in every one of his abrupt
movements. Schubert's lieder's notes, voice and piano, hanging
icicles in darkness: wonder overhead, echoed, then fled./////
How about real donkeys? If we could find one dumb enough
to starve between two bales, we would have evidence
against free will, at least as far as donkeys are concerned (or
at least that particular donkey). Staid and staying,
the biting power, the hour, the state of wait. An
analogous condition might be compulsive
metaphor-making and, perhaps, punishing
rhyme. With bitter remorse, he recalled playing piano
as a child and feeling his mother listening
behind the parlor door; he would scream annoyance
and stop practicing. Once there was a Garden
Movement. Once there were Decorative Hermits./////
June, 1920, staff open
a general store in the
basement: groceries, tobacco*

products, clothes, sewing
supplies. 1929-30,
busiest in their history;
often up to 1,000
visitors in the Main
Reading Room, SRO.
Ptolemy
studied mostly war but
became one of the greatest
cultural patrons. The Moueseion:
lecture halls, labs, guest rooms. Euclid
and Archimedes solved
problems there; Aristarchus
of Samos concluded that
the sun centered our solar system.
*For the mathematics to work, the universe would
actually consist of ten spatial dimensions:
the extra seven dimensions have rolled up out of sight.*
Y: **I left it eons ago, when radiation started
to leak.** X: **I left just now, but Ted is still back
inside.** Z *is the entanglement of all three. No drama
at the event horizon. Information loss
paradox.* They pause at their entryway, unwilling to
permit the golden dying of afternoon to relinquish
them. George Ives would have his boys sing in one key
while he accompanied in another; he built
instruments to produce quarter-tones; he played
his cornet over a pond so Charlie could gauge the effect

of space. And can we rightly speak of a beauty that is
always passing away, and is first this and then that;
must not the same thing be born and retire
and vanish while the word is in our mouths?
As George entered his house, he heard five-year old Charles
pounding out
dad's drum parts, tone clusters, on their piano with this little
fists. They are particles of each other, so they
can be transformed into each other by charge conjugation
and thus have opposite strangeness.
The computation necessary to verify
that Alice and Bob are entangled could take longer than
the age of the universe, and the black hole would
evaporate in the meantime, making it impossible
ever to go inside and experience the
contradiction. Night, an old, starved crow, memory
and instant death. There is nothing worse than a brilliant
image of a fuzzy concept. Your parents are the firm
but delicate membrane holding back a sea that hangs,
domed far above your head. Pegasus quivers in his fixed place, jetting
at some ridiculous speed, to pull beyond the sextant and the charts.
Ringlets to serpents, men to stone, the winged steed rises from
the Gorgon's blood. Anything to anything; anything from anything.
There have been greater days. Forsythia-blooms crowd
and crown our discontent. When the general
character is preserved, even if some
of the proper letters are wanting, still the thing
is signified: − well, if all the letters are given; not well,

when only a few of them are given. I think that we
had better admit this. Lest we be punished like travelers
in Aegina, who wander about the street late at night:
and be likewise told by Truth herself that we have arrived
too late. Myth is broken by the age that is sprawling
and daedalion, that has outgrown its application.
Forgiveness soaked up by a field once bright and green. Each of
the six flavors of quarks can have three different colors. The quark
forces are attractive only in colorless
combinations of three quarks (baryons), quark-antiquark
pairs (mesons), and possibly larger combinations
such as the pentaquark that could also meet the colorless
condition. Whop, whop of racquet strings against
yellow balls: too dark to really see. The gong
on the hook and ladder. The most musical town
in Connecticut. O, how be heartsick, still?/////
Theophrastus succeeded
Aristotle, his fellow
Peripatetic, in directing
the Lyceum. Having
presided for 35 years, he
died in 287, BCE, at,
some say, 107. Right
before death, he bemoaned
life's brevity — that one expires
just as one begins to
understand crucial problems.

Theophrastus objected to
certain Aristotelian
notions concerning the
existence of a Prime
Mover, as well as
universal teleology.
Mandelstam: *The past has not
even been born yet; it has
never truly come to pass.*

*I want Ovid, Pushkin, and
Catullus once more; the
historical Ovid, Pushkin
and Catullus are not
enough for me.*
AD 365, August
21, the sea abruptly
drained from Alexandria's
harbor: ships and fish left in
sand. Citizens walked into the
empty space, just before
a huge tsunami rolled over
the once-harbor, over houses
and other buildings. At least
50,000 dead. The beginning
of 200 years of
earthquakes and
rising sea levels.

Cassius Dio: *Toward
the philosophers who were called
Aristotelians, Antoninus
showed bitter hatred in every
way, even going so far
as to desire to burn their books, and
in particular he abolished
their common messes in
Alexandria and all
the other privileges that they
had enjoyed; his grievance
against them was that Aristotle
was supposed to have been concerned
in the death of Alexander.*
Researching in
wet suits the old harbor, mapping
quays, royal quarter,
perhaps the actual palace of
Cleopatra. And the
Pharos, lighthouse that once
soared forty stories. Plutarch:
*The Peripatetics no longer
possess the original texts
of Aristotle and
Theophrastus because they have
fallen into idle and base
hands.* 1911, all staff

supplied with rubber-soled
shoes because the marble floors were
deemed too hard. The O'Sullivan
Company exhorted people to
patronize the library where
employees wore the firm's product.
Left open on this
table, a book:
Think fast! *This, Mouth never
does. Thus, hurled rock takes out an
eye. Mind sends pain along. Hand tries
to touch the gone orbital.
So. But gone is gone. Now, then,
this loss is a part of me. Don't
weep, one eye. Just, more clearly, see.*/////
*Hard it is for hand to shuffle,
deal, hold, and sort. Single eye must
squint to see. Mouth, though, enjoys
this game, for a while, and
especially likes numbers, both
red and black, the only cards
Mouth receives. 3. Red. What
do they mean? 9? Black? He
loses. Pay up. But Mouth has
nothing. Then I will take that
ear. And it is gone. Mind
suspects a bad pattern.*/////

*Mouth's impoverished lease on life:
eye, ear, hand, leg now all on just
one side. Dizzy-listing, Mouth finds
it can no longer drift, yet, still
wishing to rise, searches
for leaned-already ladders.
Rung. Rung. Rung. Poor hand, leg –
nearly done for. Hoisted, finally,
to the roof, Mouth sees – no going
back: down, impossibly
harder. Leg kicks ladder away./////
On the cathedral roof, Mouth
takes stock. Clouds: gold; blood-orange. Bells
trembled by this steady
wind. Below, rough fabric of
city. In that corner,
black column of smoke rises.
Heightens. Enlarges. Approaches.
Eye twitches. Mouth wants
the ladder back./////
Tree city. Who decides? –
even this cathedral, made
of wood.* **What?** – *that expanding
wall of flame.* **Where?** – *too close, to
my high refuge.* **What?** – *being
in a pickle. So Mouth rides
roof down to ground, now cindery.*

That wall has moved past, beyond./////
Remaining eye smeared into
jelly, remaining ear
nowhere to be found, hand and
leg severed, Mouth can only
roll, hauling mind along./////
Conflagrations, that high
rock, chambers, parchments, ruins,
rivers, temples, neighborhoods,

                patience, fortitude,
grammars, bridges, lieder,
dancing, rims, religion, gulls,
silence, silliness, clothes,
crocodiles, catalogues,
asylum, ships, summits, guest
rooms, strangeness, ten
dimensions, metal on
metal, bells, fish, harbors,
ladders, drums, quays,
quarter-tones, towers: all can be
here. Here, picking up books left
by others on tables: best
books to read, beginning with
the exact pages left open.
Many leave here, a leaving that's hardly
death. Some stay, a staying that's hardly
exile, that's a welcoming of night and snow.

A Torso   (for Walter Benjamin)

Fine flag over it,
sleeping, rethinking
ground from
the ground up. Having
fallen from the train
that does not leave until
everyone is on board. A kind
of escape, at that, from its
marble block. But this
isn't narrative, not
with lightning flashes
out there and,
in here, messianic
sparks. The minor boredom
of order will come
knocking, but there isn't yet a
door in this fabric. Or
a Saturday night rolls
around like death, to cleanse
all filth from the body.
Then, maybe, chess, quick
game against that unbeatable
automaton with the
mystical dwarf hidden
inside. Seven
thimbles, 49 levels of
meaning, with nothing
seamless. *The upper
torso seems not just high, but*

blocky, huge. From Zero Zoo,
a tiger leaps into
the past: Adam, father
of philosophy, named it.
This one says, *Just wait
until daylight, and I
will go forth and learn how
to shudder. Then I shall have
a skill that will support me.*
On a stone pillow,

it waits, not
for Empty Time's
continuous flow, but –
under its flag, at
a crossroads
in the labyrinth – to see
when and where it will sit
in history, in its own
modernity that possesses
antiquity like

*a nightmare that creeps
over it.* That afternoon,
they stroll through
the arcade, sky's
narrow, gray curve
overhead. Money and
rain belong together.
The child thinks about three
bluebirds on one
branch, lunch, a map,

fox, turtle, squirrel. A
flashing at her feet. What
entrances her: *Not
what the moving neon
red sign says — but the fiery
pool reflecting it
in the asphalt.* Though what this
little one really
desires is to exit
the tunnel and, on the other side, to see the new
construction site's fine,
jagged detritus
enlivening hard-packed
earth, gigantic
dumpsters. Then
*still more men fell down, one
after the other
from the chimney. They brought
two skulls from dead men and
nine bones, then set them
up and bowled.* Lying
beyond the black, daft
border of their
territory, a dirty
heaven: young loris with
its thin shadow; *two
grains of wheat on which
a kindred soul
had inscribed the complete*

Shema Israel; pieces of toast in a playpen; white sprinkles edging a gully; taxed numbskull; blank bank; virtue mill. *Recurrence of transience, a rhythm of downfall, leading, when embraced, to great humility and to* happiness. His ability to see the remnants, the ruins inherent in grand ideas; not to deface, but to leave the face within the block; not to leave his work to become a remnant, but to fashion it, from the first, a made remnant; to remove the extraneous and leave his Atlas Slave, *imprisoned in its own body and pose, unrelieved by any opposing force.* And disruption. Rupture. A truth, *charged to the bursting point with Time.* Chip of Messianic Time,

reclaiming lost
voices. *Property
relations in Mickey
Mouse cartoons: here we
see for the first
time that it is possible
to have one's own
arm, even one's
own body, stolen.* These
prunings and the moon's

sliver should be
enough. Camp
Divine: tapestry; rhapsody; rested
quill; gym; garage; yellow
wire; vast key; outdated
globe; square fool; courtyard;
river; flight; flint;
road, with robbers *who
make an armed attack and
relieve an idler of

his convictions;*
film. *Sitting, she
helplessly stretches
her arms for a fruit that
remains beyond
her reach. And yet
she is winged. Nothing
is more true.* She, all
those leavings, ruins,
all under

a fine, blank flag that must now be a home, the new home. We have long forgotten the ritual by which the house of our life was erected.... But the human need for shelter is lasting. Architecture has never been idle. Its history is more ancient than that of any other art, and its claim to being a living force has significance in every attempt to comprehend the relationship of the masses to art. Massing under the new house. And here is a new someone. Her clothes are impermeable to every blow of fate; he looks like a man who hasn't taken his garments off for months; she is unfamiliar *with beds; when he lies down, she does so in a wheelbarrow or on a seesaw. That fine, blank flag of the Now Time. Only he who can view his own past as an abortion sprung from compulsion and need can use it to full advantage in the present. For what one has lived is at best comparable to a beautiful statue which has had all its limbs knocked off in transit, and now yields nothing but the precious block out of which the image of one's future must be hewn.*

A Ship

Its language starts to
slide: whole tale
tips; entire main
deck slightly
slants; passengers become
lovers falling into each
other's arms; their
sentences slip around,
under, into – enter.

Steerage. Once abandoned
arms hold an infant. Sick
little one cradled by hands
no longer left
behind. All that
remains is for this child
to anatomize, become
sparks rising out of
itself, out of the
hands, sight so beautiful,
disappearing into darkness.

Only that one on board
as it turns out. And after
its end – poor scrawny
thing – really everything gets
better for everybody else.
After all, children, families, do
just muck it up. Almost
impossible, with them around,
to select new loves.

There's talk of
an emptiness. A
hole all the way down
through. More like
a Mohole. More a shaft
without an
elevator, or
walls, ceiling, floor.
The closer one comes,
the colder. Not the freeze
of ice, of space. More
a ghost-bone.

Gods suddenly on board, dust
covering six bare feet. Clothes
loose fitting, thin, faded,
stained. Their spoken
thoughts hardly
celestial. Look, how
dark the water. This
journey might end. If we
may be so bold. No
berths for them; none
offered. So they huddle
close to the emptiness.

From the unseen
captain, occasionally,
an order comes down, surprising,
delightful. Today, you're
a nudist colony. You'll
switch bed partners tonight. They
glimpse no crew, but berths remain
spotless, sumptuous meals plated
and placed. They'll guess aloud about
what guides them through fogs, through
nights. Even the divinities
wonder. One says, Doubt,
too, can become a form.

Bedmates coupling or
dreaming, hearing thunder
of horses overhead. Who
are those stretched low along
straining ponies' necks? Those
who lightly hold soft,
leather reins? Who are
those who look intently
out over the onyx sea as
they circle the deck?

The celestials stumble
upon a room of maps and
charts. Curious, as ever, they
can't help but enter. One
pulls a volume from its shelf,
holds it upright, opens
randomly, and they watch
language slide down, off the
pages. A thin-lined grid, crazy
land shapes, pale green sea remain. But
words, letters fall like soot upon
and around six bare feet. Back
above, they agree to
keep this to themselves.

They claim that whirling's
their nature, that they're
doing it right now, there in
the ballroom. Why
can't we see that? someone
says. You look with eyes only. You see
threadbare motley, and six
dusty feet. You don't
perceive our hunger. You
can't discern our egos'
headstones and cerements – our
conic hats, our white robes with
skirts that lift as we turn,
left feet propelling us around
right; skirts risen, cusped
like waves, waves spinning foam off
themselves into the raven sea.

As usual, only the
deities go ashore. There,
the city's lamps blink on, skyline
scattering, softening to
lilac. They weave
along the main street, turn
to wave back, and never
disappear from sight for long.
Darkness hovers. Laughing, they
point out those most strangely garbed, new
wares on the curbs, arabesques of
lights. Quiet, at the railing,
new lovers look on.

They remember all
that uneasiness on the launch –
leaning away from touching, looking
only straight ahead, at what –
coming closer and
larger – was anchored
there, where each
would choose, as
paramour, an other.

Golden gleam of
spruce masts silk-wrapped. Starboard
cedar hull pulled open. They all
sit on narrow maple
benches and dangle, kick
pale feet in the brine. Each
looks right, left, seeking a one
and only love, for that
night. They shift places. Then,
touching of knees, thighs; stroking,
nuzzling of necks, breasts. Pirates'
lust of rubies, pearls.

Beginning, always, as
game, groping for flesh in pitch-black
corridors. Vertiginous
movements, but in a darkness
that isn't living, deep, or
blessed. Seduced through a
threshold, this one –
inconsolable, whose will's
no longer taut, whose
fidelity and charms have been
swallowed by a gulf –
slapstick-spalts into a room made –
ceiling, walls, floor – of burlap ;
the next of velvet; then of
foam. And vanishes, after
so many others. Though the
number of lovers remains
a perfect mix and match.

Sun. Sea. Lazy,
lateral rocking as it drifts
alongside a berg, size of a
holy orphanage. Couples
promenade, not a single
voyager having realized how
great the yearning for snow, until
just now, as flakes touch
lashes, cheeks, throats. Drawn
up and around them, some
massive parchment receives
its text: letters of
alabaster, pearl, eggshell,
salt, powder, frost, linen
bone, rice, lace, smoke, harp,
titan, ghost, whisper,
photon, shadow, and stone.
Beneath all this,
faces lifted into
white cold, they read
language inside out.

Growing from sky downward,
this tree, beginning
unknown, end unknowable.
It passes through on
a path to sea-bed. All those
names rustle amongst branches
in air; flicker against
walls below decks; undulate,
blur in the deep. New names
for gods, for all the
paramours. Names that cluster, rise
through and far above, then
spread into a canopy.

Word comes down of a new
museum hall. To which couples
flock, only to find that those
divine curators appear,
themselves, on exhibit, the room
otherwise empty. The trio
gesture and describe
nothingness.
     Notice bronze
hands and shoulders of this little
boy peeing into a white-tiled
font.
  Here, in marble, a
massive nude, her arm thrown
back over her unchiseled
blank of a face. Or how these
fish, with their stone tongues, leer
up from the wading pool's rim.
       And,
finally, this unicorn's
exquisite neck, that young woman's
hair falling across it, her
slender arms embracing. How
she loves the creature and wishes

that it won't leave, though also
full well knowing that it can't
be bound in any furrow.

The three speak on What
is Certainty? What is
Doubt?
 Frog spewing its rainbow
oil slick of blood.
 Swarm
of wasps not yet in focus.
 Air
growling.
 Lightning's little
tingle.
 Gold tooth flashing in
an open mouth.
 River's
current pulling a dress
tight.
 Winter's worth of
dust swirling in a room.
 Squirrel's
cheek and flank gone hollow.
 Slightest,
first gray of dawn.
 Red ghost.
 Cell
sucked down its own drain.
 This

craft, slicing sea.
                    And, sitting
before us, you
lovers, applauding.

Yet again, they file
into that ballroom, where
the divinities put on
a show. Hardly
rehearsed. First: *history, dead
people, broken things.* Looks
at piano. Second: *an
ascent, stone rung, mud rung, marble
rung, to somewhere darker
than even here.* Third:
*marble rung, stone rung, mud rung, ascent
to a room with a story that
used to be called
history.* Together: *regimes,
catastrophes, stories, words, and
we, dead except for
what we speak.* The end.

As they fade into holy
light: Should we tenderly
bestow?
          Greatheartedly
render?
          Unfurl a rumor
of destination?
                But
the more we proffer to
these wanderers, the louder
they bellow STOP!

To the crow's nest they're
invited. Only one
ascends. Between white above and
gray below, petrels and gulls;
gentle rocking starboard
to port; dreaming,
waking, dreaming of
the great mast dipping
leeward until
it submerges this arm, this
shoulder. Dreaming of falling –
with all the company –
to silence in the old
heart of the sea, of being
broken in the depths,
of becoming a
terror, then nothing.

O, to be undone seeing
the moon's beam run
its line along
blackness. O, to be
drawn beneath one watery
furrow. To be borne
upon a wing plummeting
into a night that's
the opposite of
night, where down is
the antipodean
of down, toward
an obsidian sun
that will confound and make
immune any tongue.

*On that other vessel, I opened
my mouth to scream war precisely
when an arrow pierced my
skull from above. Instantly,
a torn path through the
right periventricular
area, right frontal deep
white matter, cranial
cavity immediately
lateral to anterior
cerebral arteries, right
optic canal, right ethmoidal
and sphenoid sinuses, to
exit through point of chin. And
stopped there. The second
arrow took a simpler
route. Through right cheek, over
tongue, past that other shaft,
to exit through left cheek. And stopped
there. The battle ended, I
demanded and was brought
a full-length mirror. Leaning on
the one still-working leg, I gazed
with now just one good eye at*

*what I'd become. A tilting Celtic
cross, crucifix of
every sad, sad hour.*

The bow angel and the stern
angel ascend, helixes
of brume, rising, broadening,
silvery spirits. Now, a
slow tailwind bends,
curves them until the
one to rearward lengthens,
stretches above its other. And
they merge.

Seems there's a tunnel
after all. And
a destination. One
and the same, in fact. In
fact, one inside
the other. Ship in a
bottle. Emerald in its
velvet box. Pinkish, fading
light on deep snow at a field's
verge: that memory inside
this thought, May be the last, that's
inside this feeling – chill
spirit-breath across the
heart – inside this
event, each single
lover on board.

They wonder about
that final launch they'll board. Hope
and fear of Hurry, and
get your things. What language will
possess the air. Hills they'll stand
upon, halls inhabit. Tokens
to exchange – rings of
beaten gold or black tin, smocks
of fine holland or Scotch
cloth. The will they might
have of each other. What
dews will wet their skins; what rains
fall on their locks. And who
will let them in.

Acknowledgments

The poems in this collection, frequently in earlier versions, have appeared in *Blazing Stadium, The Brooklyn Rail, Eratio, Golden Handcuffs Review, International Times, New American Writing, Otoliths, #Ranger, Tourniquet Review,* and *Var(2x)*. Sincere thanks to the editors for their kindness to my work.

Thanks to Anton Bruckner, Mitchell Parish, Beowulf, Suzan-Lori Parks, Charles Demuth, Hector Berlioz, Richard Strauss, Will Kimball, Albrecht Glockenton, *Indian Summer: The Cannonsville Story* – directed by Jules Victor Schwerin, DEP Police Records, Bob Reinhardt, Hogarth, Lucan, New York Public Library.org, Osip Mandelstam, Cassius Dio, Plutarch, Brothers Grimm, Paul Hansen, Walter Benjamin, David Lynch, Bertolt Brecht, "The Lass of Aughrim" lyricist, for your lives, and for references to and quotations from your thoughts and works.

About the Author

JOEL CHACE hails from Upstate New York. After thirty-eight years of teaching literature and creative writing in schools around the world, he is now retired and living with his wife in Lancaster, Pennsylvania. He has published work in print and electronic magazines such as *Tip of the Knife*, *Eratio*, *Otoliths*, *Word For/Word*, *Golden Handcuffs Review*, *New American Writing*, and *The Brooklyn Rail*. His full-length collections include *matter no matter*, from Paper Kite Press, *Humors*, from Paloma Press, *Threnodies*, from Moria Books, *fata morgana*, from Unlikely Books, and *Maths*, from Chax Press. Chace is an NEH Fellow.

www.ingramcontent.com/pod-product-compliance
Lightning Source LLC
Chambersburg PA
CBHW020335170426
43200CB00006B/397

Praise for *Underrated Provinces*

Nation is a fragile construct, and rarely more fragile than in Joel Chace's tensive, meditative lyrics. Placemaking and placelessness jostle here as songlines torn from a past that is never quite done thinking of us. Chace's lyrics hang in fixed frames like paintings on a wall—here is a village flooded by a hydro project; here is a library; here is a trombone—even as they collate the disparate voices of a United States sliding into representations of itself. In *Underrated Provinces*, the mouth calls nothing home except the voice that escapes it.

—G. C. Waldrep, author of *The Earliest Witnesses*

Joel Chace's astounding taut-lined *Underrated Provinces* seems a coat hung on a point of light in one of history's dark maneuvers. It's a triumph to be savored again and again.

—Noelle Kocot, author of *Poem for the End of Time and Other Poems* and *Ascent of the Mothers*

Underrated Provinces takes us into an arresting dream vision of a drowned and burning world, and sets sail. Words bubble up from the page in uncanny spaces, through door frames, halls and school rooms, in translations of grain elevators, the making and unmaking of towns and canals. This is America as reverie, shaped by the forces of living architecture, in headlong transit amongst the ruins of the future, with the resources of the past—ancient lost libraries, painting, song, music—scattered, beautiful and strange. What will it mean to find a mouth to say it? What new language will possess the air? And as they travel, who will let them in?

—Carol Watts, author of *Occasionals*, *When Blue Light Falls*, and *Kelptown*